# THE *Skinny*
# NUTRiBULLET
## RECIPE BOOK

CookNation

# THE SKINNY NUTRIBULLET RECIPE BOOK
## 80+ DELICIOUS & NUTRITIOUS HEALTHY SMOOTHIE RECIPES. BURN FAT, LOSE WEIGHT AND FEEL GREAT!

**ISBN 978-1-909855-57-1**

A CIP catalogue record of this book is available from the British Library

• • • • • • • • • • • • • • • • • • • • • • • • • • • • • • • • • • • • • • • • • • • • • • • • • • • •

## DISCLAIMER

# CONTENTS

# GREEN SMOOTHIES

# You may also enjoy.....

DELICIOUS, QUICK & EASY, SINGLE
SERVING SOUPS & PASTA SAUCES
FOR YOUR NUTRIBULLET.
ALL UNDER 100, 200, 300 & 400
CALORIES

ISBN 978-1-909855-59-5

QUICK & EASY, SINGLE SERVING
SUPPERS, SNACKS, SAUCES,
SALAD DRESSINGS & MORE USING
YOUR NUTRIBULLET. ALL UNDER
300, 400 & 500 CALORIES

ISBN 978-1-909855-65-6

# INTRODUCTION

## Just one Nutriblast a day can make a difference to the way you feel and it only takes seconds to make!

If you are reading this you will likely already have purchased a NUTRiBULLET or perhaps are considering buying one. A smart choice! The NUTRiBULLET is unquestionably one of the highest performing smoothie creators on the market. Its clean lines and compact design look great in any kitchen. It's simple to use, easy to clean and the results are amazing.

You may have watched or read some of the NUTRiBULLET marketing videos and literature which make claims of using the power of the NUTRiBULLET to help you lose weight, boost your immune system and fight a number of ailments and diseases. Of course the 'healing' power comes from the foods we use to make our smoothies but the real difference with the NUTRiBULLET is that it EXTRACTS all the goodness of the ingredients. Unlike many juicers and blenders, which leave behind valuable fibre, the NUTRiBULLET pulverizes the food, breaking down their cell walls and unlocking the valuable nutrients so your body can absorb and use them.

You may have made your own smoothies in the past using a blender – you'll know even with a powerful device that there are often indigestible pieces of food left in your glass – not so with the NUTRiBULLET which uses 600 watts to breakdown every part of the food. The manufacturer calls it 'cyclonic action' running at 10,000 revolutions per minute but whatever the marketing jargon, the results speak for themselves.

The NUTRiBULLET is not a blender and not a juicer. It is a nutrient extractor, getting the very best from every ingredient you put in and delivering a nutrient packed Nutriblast.

## THERE HAS NEVER BEEN A BETTER TIME to introduce health-boosting, weight reducing and well-being smoothies to your life. With a spiralling obesity epidemic in the western world which in turn is linked to a growing list of debilitating diseases and ailments including diabetes, high blood pressure, heart disease, high cholesterol, infertility, skin conditions and more, the future for many of us can look bleak. Combine this with the super-fast pace of modern life and we can be left feeling fatigued and lethargic, worsened by daily consumption of unhealthy foods.

Using the power from a nutrient packed Nutriblast is an incredibly fast and efficient way of giving our bodies the goodness they need. Making the most of anti-oxidants to protect your cells, omega 3 fatty acids to help your joints, fibre to aid digestion and protein to build and repair muscles.

Just one Nutriblast a day can make a difference to the way you feel and it only takes seconds to make!

# NUTRIBLASTS FOR WEIGHT LOSS

Drinking Nutriblasts for weight loss can be a great way to aid a diet or weight management program. Our delicious recipes are packed with healthy ingredients, which will help you achieve your recommended daily quota of fruit and veg, yet are light on calories. Replacing just one meal a day with one of our weight loss Nutriblasts will leave you feeling satisfied, knowing that the goodness in a glass is packed with nutrient dense ingredients. By stripping your diet of unhealthy processed foods weight loss becomes effortless and within days you'll feel brighter, stronger, more energetic and focussed.

**The Skinny NUTRiBULLET Recipe book** is packed with over 80 delicious and simple recipes.

......................................................................................

## Benefits can include:

## WEIGHT LOSS · REJUVENATION · GLOWING SKIN · INCREASED ENERGY · LOWER BLOOD PRESSURE · LOWER CHOLESTEROL

## and overall enhanced wellbeing.

......................................................................................

All our recipes make use of the tall cup of the NUTRiBULLET and the extractor blade. We encourage you to experiment with your Nutriblasts, mixing your ingredients is fun and will help your create wonderful new 'blasts'. As a basic formula work on 50% leafy greens 50% fruit, ¼ cup of seeds/nuts and water.
**We hope you enjoy our recipes.**

## TIPS

To help make your Nutriblast fuss-free, follow these quick tips.

- Prepare your shopping list. Take some time to select which Nutriblasts you want to prepare in advance. As with all food shopping, make a note of all the ingredients and quantities you need. Depending on the ingredients it's best not to shop too far in advance to ensure you are getting the freshest produce available. We recommend buying organic produce whenever you can if your budget allows. Organic produce can give a better yield and flavour to your Nutriblast. Remember almost all fruit is fine to freeze too.
- Wash your fruit and veg before juicing. This needn't take up much time but all produce should be washed clean of any traces of bacteria, pesticides and insects.
- To save time prepare produce the night before for early morning Nutriblasts.
- Cut up any produce that may not fit into the tall cup, but only do this just before juicing to keep it as fresh as possible.

- Wash your Nutriblast parts immediately after juicing.  As tempting as it may be to leave it till a little later you'll be glad you took the few minutes to rinse and wash before any residue has hardened.
- Substitute where you need to.  If you can't source a particular ingredient, try another instead.  More often than not you will find the use of a different fruit or veg makes a really interesting and delicious alternative.  In our recipes we offer some advice on alternatives but have the confidence to make your own too!
- Some Nutriblasts are sweeter than others and it's a fact that some of the leafy green drinks can take a little getting used to. Try drinking these with a straw, you'll find them easier to drink and enjoy.
- Drink lots of water!

## IMPORTANT – WHAT NOT TO USE IN YOUR NUTRIBLASTS

The manufacturers of NUTRiBULLET are very clear on the following warning.  While the joy of making Nutriblasts is using whole fruit and vegetables there are a few seeds and pits which should be removed. The following contain chemicals which can release cyanide into the body when ingested so do not use any of the following in your Nutriblasts:

- **Apple Seeds**
- **Apricot Pits**
- **Cherry Pits**
- **Plum Pits**
- **Peach pits**

## CLEANING

Cleaning the NUTRiBULLET is thankfully very easy.  The manufacturer gives clear guidelines on how best to do this but here's a recap:

Make sure the NUTRiBULLET is unplugged before disassembling or cleaning.
Set aside the power base and blade holders as these should not be used in a dishwasher.
Use hot soapy water to clean the blades but do not immerse in boiling water as this can warp the plastic.

Use a damp cloth to clean the power base.
All cups and lids can be placed in a dishwasher.
For stubborn marks inside the cup, fill the cup 2/3 full of warm soapy water and screw on the milling blade.
Attached to the power base and run for 20-30 seconds.

## WARNING:

Do not put your hands or any utensils near the moving blade.  Always ensure the NUTRiBULLET is unplugged when assembling/disassembling or cleaning.

## ABOUT COOKNATION

CookNation is the leading publisher of innovative and practical recipe books for the modern, health conscious cook.

CookNation titles bring together delicious, easy and practical recipes with their unique approach - easy and delicious, no-nonsense recipes - making cooking for diets and healthy eating fast, simple and fun.

With a range of #1 best-selling titles - from the innovative 'Skinny' calorie-counted series, to the 5:2 Diet Recipes collection - CookNation recipe books prove that 'Diet' can still mean 'Delicious'!

Turn to the end of this book to browse all CookNation's recipe books

 **CookNation**

# Skinny
# NUTRiBLASTS

# GINGER & BLUEBERRY BLAST

**SERVES 1**
NUTRiBLAST

## Ingredients

**REFRESHING TASTE!**

- 2 handfuls of spinach
- 1 fresh medium beetroot
- 1 banana
- 100g/3½oz blueberries
- 2cm/1 inch fresh ginger root
- Water

## Method

**1** Rinse the ingredients well.

**2** Cut the green stalks off the beetroot and dice.

**3** Peel the banana and break into three pieces.

**4** Add all the fruit & vegetables to the NUTRiBULLET tall cup. Make sure the ingredients do not go past the MAX line on your machine.

**5** Add water, again being careful not to exceed the MAX line.

**6** Twist on the NUTRiBULLET blade and blend until smooth.

### CHEF'S NOTE
Optional Nutriboost: Add 1 teaspoon flax seeds.

# BERRY & CINNAMON BLAST

## Ingredients

- 2 handfuls of spinach
- 1 banana
- 125g/4oz strawberries
- 125g/4oz raspberries
- 125g/4oz fresh peeled pineapple
- 1 tsp ground cinnamon
- Water

## Method

**1** Rinse the ingredients well.

**2** Peel the banana and break into three pieces.

**3** Cut the green tops of the strawberries.

**4** Add the fruit, vegetables & ground cinnamon to the NUTRiBULLET tall cup. Make sure the ingredients do not go past the MAX line on your machine.

**5** Add water, again being careful not to exceed the MAX line.

**6** Twist on the NUTRiBULLET blade and blend until smooth.

### CHEF'S NOTE
Feel free to experiment with the cinnamon quantity in this recipe - you may prefer a little less.

# ALMOND MILK & BEETROOT BLAST

## Ingredients

**SWEET & NUTTY!**

- 1 fresh large beetroot
- 1 orange
- 200g/7oz mixed berries
- 120ml/½ cup almond milk
- 1 tbsp runny honey
- 1 handful fresh walnuts
- Water

## Method

**1** Rinse the ingredients well.

**2** Cut the green stalks off the beetroot and dice.

**3** Peel the orange and separate into segments.

**4** Add the fruit, vegetables, milk, honey & walnuts to the NUTRiBULLET tall cup. Make sure the ingredients do not go past the MAX line on your machine.

**5** Add water, again being careful not to exceed the MAX line.

**6** Twist on the NUTRiBULLET blade and blend until smooth.

### CHEF'S NOTE
The fresh walnuts should be shelled before adding to the cup.

14

# COCONUT & KALE BLAST

## Ingredients

- 2 handfuls of kale
- 1 apple
- 1 banana

- 1 tsp ground cinnamon
- 250ml/1 cup coconut water

## Method

**1** Rinse the ingredients well.

**2** Core the apple, leaving the skin on. Peel the banana and break into three pieces.

**3** Add all the ingredients to the NUTRiBULLET tall cup. Making sure they do not go past the MAX line on your machine.

**4** Twist on the NUTRiBULLET blade and blend until smooth.

### CHEF'S NOTE
Use as much coconut milk as you need to fill to the max.

# SPINACH, PINEAPPLE & COCONUT WATER BLAST

## Ingredients

**LIGHT & FRESH!**

- 2 handfuls of spinach
- 1 celery stalk
- 1 banana
- 200g/7oz fresh pineapple
- 250ml/1 cup coconut water

## Method

**1** Rinse the ingredients well.

**2** Chop the celery stalk. Peel the banana and break into three pieces.

**3** Add all the ingredients to the NUTRiBULLET tall cup. Making sure they do not go past the MAX line on your machine.

**4** Twist on the NUTRiBULLET blade and blend until smooth.

### CHEF'S NOTE
A handful of acai berries makes a great boost to this Nutriblast.

# CHIA SEED & CUCUMBER BLAST

## Ingredients

- 2 handfuls of spinach
- 1 apple
- 1 banana
- ½ cucumber
- 1 tsp chia seeds
- 2 tbsp rolled oats
- Water

## Method

**1** Rinse the ingredients well.

**2** Core the apple, leaving the skin on. Peel the banana and break into three pieces.

**3** Dice the cucumber, leaving the skin on.

**4** Add the fruit, vegetables, chia seeds & oats to the NUTRiBULLET tall cup. Make sure the ingredients do not go past the MAX line on your machine.

**5** Add water, again being careful not to exceed the MAX line.

**6** Twist on the NUTRiBULLET blade and blend until smooth.

## CHEF'S NOTE

Flax seeds make a good alternative to chia seeds in this Nutriblast.

# TROPICAL FRUIT & FLAX BLAST

## Ingredients

 **NUTRIBOOST +**

- 2 handfuls of spinach
- 1 kiwi fruit
- 125g/4oz fresh mango
- 1 banana
- 1 carrot
- 1-2 tsp of flax seeds
- Water

## Method

**1** Rinse the ingredients well.

**2** Peel & dice the kiwi. De-stone and peel the mango. Peel the banana and break into three pieces.

**3** Scrub the carrot. Remove the top and slice.

**4** Add the fruit, vegetables & flax seeds to the NUTRiBULLET tall cup. Make sure the ingredients do not go past the MAX line on your machine.

**5** Add water, again being careful not to exceed the MAX line.

**6** Twist on the NUTRiBULLET blade and blend until smooth.

### CHEF'S NOTE
You could substitute coconut water for regular water in this Nutriblast.

# DOUBLE GREEN NUT BLAST

## Ingredients

- 1 handful of kale
- 2 handfuls of spinach
- 1 apple
- 1 banana
- ¼ cantaloupe melon
- 1 handful of cashew nuts
- Water

## Method

**1** Rinse the ingredients well.

**2** Core the apple, leaving the skin on. Peel the banana and break into three pieces.

**3** Scoop out the melon flesh, discarding the seeds & rind.

**4** Add the fruit, vegetables & nuts to the NUTRiBULLET tall cup. Make sure the ingredients do not go past the MAX line on your machine.

**5** Add water, again being careful not to exceed the MAX line.

**6** Twist on the NUTRiBULLET blade and blend until smooth.

### CHEF'S NOTE
Try almonds or walnuts in place of the cashew nuts.

# HARD-CORE GREEN BLAST

**SERVES 1**
NUTRiBLAST

## Ingredients

**DETOX JUICE** →

- 2 handfuls of spinach
- 2 handfuls of kale
- 1 apple
- 1 banana
- 125g/4oz green beans
- Water

## Method

**1** Rinse the ingredients well.

**2** Core the apple, leaving the skin on. Peel the banana and break into three pieces.

**3** Add all the fruit & vegetables to the NUTRiBULLET tall cup. Make sure the ingredients do not go past the MAX line on your machine.

**4** Add water, again being careful not to exceed the MAX line.

**5** Twist on the NUTRiBULLET blade and blend until smooth.

### CHEF'S NOTE
Reduce the kale quantity if you aren't ready for hard-core greens!

# CREAMY AVOCADO MORNING BLAST

## Ingredients

- 2 handfuls of spinach
- 1 avocado
- 1 apple
- 1 banana
- 1-2 tsp of flax seeds
- Water

## Method

**1** Rinse the ingredients well.

**2** Scoop out the avocado flesh discarding the rind & stone.

**3** Core the apple, leaving the skin on. Peel the banana and break into three pieces.

**4** Add the fruit, vegetables & flax seeds to the NUTRiBULLET tall cup. Make sure the ingredients do not go past the MAX line on your machine.

**5** Add water, again being careful not to exceed the MAX line.

**6** Twist on the NUTRiBULLET blade and blend until smooth.

### CHEF'S NOTE
Try pumpkin seeds or sesame seeds as an alternative to flax seeds.

# ORANGE & ALMOND MILK BLAST

## Ingredients

GOOD FOR SKIN! ➡

- 2 handfuls of spinach
- 1 orange
- 1 apple
- 120ml/½ cup almond milk
- 1 tbsp runny honey
- Water

## Method

**1** Rinse the ingredients well.

**2** Peel the orange and separate into segments.

**3** Core the apple, leaving the skin on

**4** Add the fruit, vegetables, milk & honey to the NUTRiBULLET tall cup. Make sure the ingredients do not go past the MAX line on your machine.

**5** Add water (if there is space), again being careful not to exceed the MAX line.

**6** Twist on the NUTRiBULLET blade and blend until smooth.

### CHEF'S NOTE
Optional Nutriboost: Add 2 teaspoons of sunflower seeds.

# BANANA & ALMOND BLAST

## Ingredients

- 2 handfuls of shredded romaine lettuce
- 1 pear
- 2 bananas
- 1 handful shelled almonds
- Water

## Method

**1** Rinse the ingredients well.

**2** Core the pear, leaving the skin on. Peel the bananas and break into three pieces each.

**3** Add the fruit, vegetables & almonds to the NUTRiBULLET tall cup. Make sure the ingredients do not go past the MAX line on your machine.

**4** Add water, again being careful not to exceed the MAX line.

**5** Twist on the NUTRiBULLET blade and blend until smooth.

## CHEF'S NOTE

Optional Nutriboost: Add 1 teaspoon of hemp seeds.

# LEMON & MINT, COCONUT MILK BLAST

## Ingredients

**VITAMIN 'C' +**

- 2 handfuls of shredded romaine lettuce
- 1 apple
- ½ lemon
- ¼ cucumber
- 1 tbsp chopped fresh mint
- 250ml/1 cup coconut water

## Method

**1** Rinse the ingredients well.

**2** Core the apple, leaving the skin on. Peel the lemon; don't worry about removing the pips.

**3** Dice the cucumber, leaving the skin on.

**4** Add all the ingredients to the NUTRiBULLET tall cup. Making sure they do not go past the MAX line on your machine.

**5** Twist on the NUTRiBULLET blade and blend until smooth.

### CHEF'S NOTE
Use as much coconut milk as you need to fill to the max line.

# FRUITY CHARD BLAST

## Ingredients

- 2 handfuls of Swiss chard
- 1 banana
- 200g/7oz fresh peeled pineapple
- 1 handful of shelled almonds
- Water

## Method

1 Rinse the ingredients well.

2 Peel the banana and break into three pieces.

3 Add the fruit, vegetables & almonds to the NUTRiBULLET tall cup. Make sure the ingredients do not go past the MAX line on your machine.

4 Add water, again being careful not to exceed the MAX line.

5 Twist on the NUTRiBULLET blade and blend until smooth.

## CHEF'S NOTE
Optional Nutriboost: Add 1 tablespoon of goji berries.

# WALNUT & AVOCADO, BERRY BLAST

## Ingredients

**EXTRA CREAMY!**

- 2 handfuls of spinach
- ½ avocado
- 1 banana
- 200g/7oz blueberries
- 1 tsp runny honey
- 1 handful of shelled walnuts
- Water

## Method

**1** Rinse the ingredients well.

**2** Scoop out the avocado flesh, discarding the stone and skin.

**3** Peel the banana and break into three pieces.

**4** Add the fruit, vegetables, honey & nuts to the NUTRiBULLET tall cup. Make sure the ingredients do not go past the MAX line on your machine.

**5** Add water, again being careful not to exceed the MAX line.

**6** Twist on the NUTRiBULLET blade and blend until smooth.

### CHEF'S NOTE
Add a little more honey if you want it sweeter!

# DOUBLE SEED PINEAPPLE BOOST

## Ingredients

- 2 handfuls of spinach
- 1 banana
- 200g/7oz fresh peeled pineapple
- 1 tsp each flax & chia seeds
- Water

## Method

**1** Rinse the ingredients well.

**2** Peel the banana and break into three pieces.

**3** Add the fruit, vegetables & seeds to the NUTRiBULLET tall cup. Make sure the ingredients do not go past the MAX line on your machine.

**4** Add water, again being careful not to exceed the MAX line.

**5** Twist on the NUTRiBULLET blade and blend until smooth.

### CHEF'S NOTE
You could also try this with a little almond milk or coconut water.

# CARROT & BERRY BLAST

**SERVES 1**
NUTRiBLAST

## Ingredients

**VITAMIN 'A' SOURCE** →

- 2 handfuls of spinach
- 2 carrots
- 200g/7oz mixed berries
- 120ml/½ cup almond milk
- Water

## Method

**1** Rinse the ingredients well.

**2** Scrub and slice the carrots, discarding the tops.

**3** Add the fruit, vegetables & almond milk to the NUTRiBULLET tall cup. Make sure the ingredients do not go past the MAX line on your machine.

**4** Add water, (if there is space) again being careful not to exceed the MAX line.

**5** Twist on the NUTRiBULLET blade and blend until smooth.

### CHEF'S NOTE
Optional Nutriboost: Add 1 tablespoon of pumpkin seeds.

# LEMON & GINGER BLAST

## Ingredients

- 2 handfuls of spinach
- ½ lemon
- 1 banana
- 200g/7oz fresh peeled pineapple
- 2cm/1 inch fresh ginger root
- Water

## Method

**1** Rinse the ingredients well.

**2** Peel the lemon, don't worry about the pips. Peel the banana and break into three pieces.

**3** Add all the fruit & vegetables to the NUTRiBULLET tall cup. Make sure the ingredients do not go past the MAX line on your machine.

**4** Add water, again being careful not to exceed the MAX line.

**5** Twist on the NUTRiBULLET blade and blend until smooth.

### CHEF'S NOTE
Optional Nutriboost: Add 1 teaspoon of hemp seeds.

# GOJI BERRY BLAST

## Ingredients

**NUTRIBOOST +**

- 2 handfuls of spinach or spring greens
- 125g/4oz strawberries
- 1 banana
- 2 tbsp goji berries
- 120ml/½ cup almond milk
- Water

## Method

**1** Rinse the ingredients well.

**2** Cut the green tops off the strawberries.

**3** Peel the banana and break into three pieces.

**4** Add the fruit, vegetables & milk to the NUTRiBULLET tall cup. Make sure the ingredients do not go past the MAX line on your machine.

**5** Add water (if there's space), again being careful not to exceed the MAX line.

**6** Twist on the NUTRiBULLET blade and blend until smooth.

### CHEF'S NOTE
Optional Nutriboost: Add 1 teaspoon of sunflower seeds.

# LIGHT SPRING BLAST

## Ingredients

- 1 handful of spring greens
- 1 handful of shredded romaine lettuce
- 1 pear
- 1 banana
- Water

## Method

**1** Rinse the ingredients well.

**2** Core the pear, leaving the skin on. Peel the banana and break into three pieces.

**3** Add all the fruit & vegetables to the NUTRiBULLET tall cup. Make sure the ingredients do not go past the MAX line on your machine.

**4** Add water, again being careful not to exceed the MAX line.

**5** Twist on the NUTRiBULLET blade and blend until smooth.

### CHEF'S NOTE
Optional Nutriboost: Add 1 tablespoon of acai berries.

# SIMPLE STRAWBERRY & SPINACH BLAST

## Ingredients

**QUICK & EASY!**

- **2 handfuls of spinach**
- **1 banana**
- **250g/9oz strawberries**
- **Water**

## Method

**1** Rinse the ingredients well.

**2** Peel the banana and break into three pieces.

**3** Cut the green tops of the strawberries.

**4** Add all the fruit & vegetables to the NUTRiBULLET tall cup. Make sure the ingredients do not go past the MAX line on your machine.

**5** Add water, again being careful not to exceed the MAX line.

**6** Twist on the NUTRiBULLET blade and blend until smooth.

### CHEF'S NOTE
Optional Nutriboost: Add 1 teaspoon of flax seeds.

# KALE, BEETROOT & MANGO BOOST

## Ingredients

- 2 handfuls of kale
- 1 pear
- 1 apple
- 1 small fresh beetroot
- 100g/3½oz fresh mango
- Water

## Method

**1** Rinse the ingredients well.

**2** Core the pear and apple, leaving the skin on.

**3** Remove and discard the green tops from the beetroot, cube the bulb. Peel the mango, discard the stone.

**4** Add all the fruit & vegetables to the NUTRiBULLET tall cup. Make sure the ingredients do not go past the MAX line on your machine.

**5** Add water, again being careful not to exceed the MAX line.

**6** Twist on the NUTRiBULLET blade and blend until smooth.

### CHEF'S NOTE
Kale is one of the more 'hard-core' greens. You could substitute for spinach or lettuce if you wish.

# SWEET POTATO & ALMOND BLAST

**SERVES 1**
NUTRiBLAST

## Ingredients

LOW CHOLESTEROL →

- 2 handfuls of spinach
- 150g/5oz sweet potatoes
- Pinch of ground nutmeg
- 120ml/½ cup almond milk
- 1 tsp runny honey
- Water

## Method

**1** Rinse the ingredients well.

**2** Cube the sweet potatoes, leaving the skin on.

**3** Add the vegetables, nutmeg, milk & honey to the NUTRiBULLET tall cup. Make sure the ingredients do not go past the MAX line on your machine.

**4** Add water (if there's space), again being careful not to exceed the MAX line.

**5** Twist on the NUTRiBULLET blade and blend until smooth.

### CHEF'S NOTE
Optional Nutriboost: Add 1 tablespoon of shelled fresh walnuts.

# BROCCOLI & SWEET CARROT BLAST

## Ingredients

- 1 handful shredded lettuce
- 150g/5oz tenderstem broccoli
- 1 apple
- 1 banana
- 1 carrot
- Water

- 1 handful shredded lettuce
- 150g/5oz tenderstem broccoli
- 1 apple
- 1 banana
- 1 carrot
- Water

## Method

**1** Rinse the ingredients well.

**2** Chop the broccoli into chunks.

**3** Core the apple, leaving the skin on. Peel the banana and break into three pieces.

**4** Scrub the carrot. Discard the top and chop into chunks.

**5** Add all the fruit & vegetables to the NUTRiBULLET tall cup. Make sure the ingredients do not go past the MAX line on your machine.

**6** Add water, again being careful not to exceed the MAX line.

**7** Twist on the NUTRiBULLET blade and blend until smooth.

### CHEF'S NOTE

Optional Nutriboost: Add 1 tablespoon of fresh cashew nuts.

# NUTTY PEACH BLAST

## Ingredients

**GOOD FATS** →

- 2 handfuls of spinach
- 1 banana
- 1 peach
- 2 handfuls of fresh cashew nuts
- Water

## Method

**1** Rinse the ingredients well.

**2** Peel the banana and break into three pieces.

**3** De-stone the peach, leaving the skin on.

**4** Add all the fruit, vegetables & nuts to the NUTRiBULLET tall cup. Make sure the ingredients do not go past the MAX line on your machine.

**5** Add water, again being careful not to exceed the MAX line.

**6** Twist on the NUTRiBULLET blade and blend until smooth.

### CHEF'S NOTE
Feel free to experiment with the water and nut quantities to get the consistency to your liking.

# HONEY & GRAPEFRUIT BLAST

## Ingredients

- 2 handfuls of spinach
- 1 grapefruit
- 200g/7oz fresh peeled pineapple
- 1 tbsp runny honey
- Water

## Method

**1** Rinse the ingredients well.

**2** Peel the grapefruit and divide into segments, don't worry about the pips.

**3** Add all the fruit & vegetables to the NUTRiBULLET tall cup. Make sure the ingredients do not go past the MAX line on your machine.

**4** Add water, again being careful not to exceed the MAX line.

**5** Twist on the NUTRiBULLET blade and blend until smooth.

### CHEF'S NOTE
Optional Nutriboost: Add 1 teaspoon of sunflower seeds.

# GRAPE & GREENS BLAST

## Ingredients

**RICH IN IRON**

- 2 handfuls of spinach or kale
- 1 pear
- 1 apple
- 200g/7oz fresh seedless green grapes
- Water

## Method

**1** Rinse the ingredients well.

**2** Core the pear and apple, leaving the skin on.

**3** Remove any stalks from the grapes.

**4** Add all the fruit & vegetables to the NUTRiBULLET tall cup. Make sure the ingredients do not go past the MAX line on your machine.

**5** Add water, again being careful not to exceed the MAX line.

**6** Twist on the NUTRiBULLET blade and blend until smooth.

## CHEF'S NOTE
For a thicker Nutriblast add a banana.

# BROCCOLI & BANANA CHIA BLAST

## Ingredients

- 250g/9oz tenderstem broccoli
- 2 bananas
- 1-2 tsp chia seeds
- Water

## Method

**1** Rinse the ingredients well.

**2** Chop the broccoli into chunks.

**3** Peel the bananas and break into three pieces each.

**4** Add the fruit, vegetables & chia seeds to the NUTRiBULLET tall cup. Make sure the ingredients do not go past the MAX line on your machine.

**5** Add water, again being careful not to exceed the MAX line.

**6** Twist on the NUTRiBULLET blade and blend until smooth.

### CHEF'S NOTE
Purple sprouting broccoli & tenderstem broccoli have a lovely natural sweetness.

# MEGA BREAKFAST BLAST

**SERVES 1**
NUTRiBLAST

## Ingredients

**NATURALLY SWEET!**

- 1 handful of spinach
- 1 pear
- 1 apple
- 1 banana
- 1 handful fresh, shelled almonds
- 1 tbsp rolled oats
- 1 tbsp runny honey
- Water

## Method

**1** Rinse the ingredients well.

**2** Core the pear and apple, leaving the skin on. Peel the banana and break into three pieces.

**3** Add the fruit, vegetables, oats & honey to the NUTRiBULLET tall cup. Make sure the ingredients do not go past the MAX line on your machine.

**4** Add water, again being careful not to exceed the MAX line.

**5** Twist on the NUTRiBULLET blade and blend until smooth.

### CHEF'S NOTE
Optional Nutriboost: Add 1 teaspoon of hemp seeds.

# APPLE CHERRY BLAST

## Ingredients

- 2 handfuls of spinach
- 1 apple
- 1 banana
- 200g/7oz pitted cherries
- Water

## Method

**1** Rinse the ingredients well.

**2** Core the apple, leaving the skin on. Peel the banana and break into three pieces.

**3** Ensure the cherries are free from pips and stalks.

**4** Add all the fruit & vegetables to the NUTRiBULLET tall cup. Make sure the ingredients do not go past the MAX line on your machine.

**5** Add water, again being careful not to exceed the MAX line.

**6** Twist on the NUTRiBULLET blade and blend until smooth.

### CHEF'S NOTE
Optional Nutriboost: Add 1 teaspoon of flax seeds.

41

# CARROT & TURMERIC BLAST

## Ingredients

**CURCUMIN SOURCE** →

- 2 handfuls of spinach
- 2 carrots
- 1 banana
- ½ tsp turmeric
- Water

## Method

**1** Rinse the ingredients well.

**2** Scrub the carrots, discarding the tops before chopping.

**3** Peel the banana and break into three pieces.

**4** Add the fruit, vegetables & turmeric to the NUTRiBULLET tall cup. Make sure the ingredients do not go past the MAX line on your machine.

**5** Add water, again being careful not to exceed the MAX line.

**6** Twist on the NUTRiBULLET blade and blend until smooth.

### CHEF'S NOTE
Turmeric can stain cooking equipment, so make sure you wash everything straight away.

# PAPAYA & PINEAPPLE BLAST

## Ingredients

- 1 handful of spinach
- 1 banana
- ½ small papaya fruit
- 150g/5oz fresh peeled pineapple
- Water

## Method

**1** Rinse the ingredients well.

**2** Peel the banana and break into three pieces.

**3** Scoop out the papaya flesh, discarding the seeds and rind.

**4** Add all the fruit & vegetables to the NUTRiBULLET tall cup. Make sure the ingredients do not go past the MAX line on your machine.

**5** Add water, again being careful not to exceed the MAX line.

**6** Twist on the NUTRiBULLET blade and blend until smooth.

## CHEF'S NOTE
Optional Nutriboost: Add 1 teaspoon of chia or flax seeds.

# ZUCCHINI & CUCUMBER BLAST

## Ingredients

**VITAMIN 'B' +**

- 1 handful of spinach or kale
- 1 courgette
- ½ cucumber
- 1 apple
- Water

## Method

**1** Rinse the ingredients well.

**2** Top and tail the courgette & cucumber, leaving the skin on.

**3** Core the apple, leaving the skin on.

**4** Add all the fruit & vegetables to the NUTRiBULLET tall cup. Make sure the ingredients do not go past the MAX line on your machine.

**5** Add water, again being careful not to exceed the MAX line.

**6** Twist on the NUTRiBULLET blade and blend until smooth.

### CHEF'S NOTE
Add ½ peeled lemon for a brighter blast!

# MINTED ORANGE BLAST

## Ingredients

- 2 handfuls of shredded romaine lettuce
- 2 oranges
- 1 carrot
- 1 tbsp chopped fresh mint
- Water

## Method

**1** Rinse the ingredients well.

**2** Peel the oranges and separate into segments, don't worry about the pips.

**3** Scrub the carrots, removing and discarding the tops before chopping.

**4** Add all the fruit & vegetables to the NUTRiBULLET tall cup. Make sure the ingredients do not go past the MAX line on your machine.

**5** Add water, again being careful not to exceed the MAX line.

**6** Twist on the NUTRiBULLET blade and blend until smooth.

### CHEF'S NOTE
Optional Nutriboost: Add 1 tablespoon of fresh almonds.

# CRANBERRY CRUSH

## Ingredients

VITAMIN 'C'+'E'

- 2 handfuls of shredded romaine lettuce
- 1 apple
- ½ lime
- 1 banana
- 200g/7oz fresh cranberries
- Water

## Method

**1** Rinse the ingredients well.

**2** Core the apple, leaving the skin on. Peel the lime, don't worry about the pips.

**3** Add all the fruit & vegetables to the NUTRiBULLET tall cup. Make sure the ingredients do not go past the MAX line on your machine.

**4** Add water, again being careful not to exceed the MAX line.

**5** Twist on the NUTRiBULLET blade and blend until smooth.

### CHEF'S NOTE
Optional Nutriboost: Add 1 tablespoon of acai berries.

# SUPER SALAD

## Ingredients

- 2 handfuls of shredded romaine lettuce
- 2 celery stalks
- ¼ cucumber
- ¼ lemon
- 1 vine ripened tomato
- Water

## Method

**1** Rinse the ingredients well.

**2** Peel the lemon, don't worry about the pips.

**3** Discard the tomato stalk and cut into quarters.

**4** Add all the fruit & vegetables to the NUTRiBULLET tall cup. Make sure the ingredients do not go past the MAX line on your machine.

**5** Add water, again being careful not to exceed the MAX line.

**6** Twist on the NUTRiBULLET blade and blend until smooth.

### CHEF'S NOTE
Optional Nutriboost: Add 1 teaspoon sunflower seeds.

# BASIL & LIME APPLE BLAST

## Ingredients

VITAMIN 'K'

- 2 handfuls of spinach
- 2 apples
- ½ lime
- 2 tbsp fresh chopped basil
- Water

## Method

**1** Rinse the ingredients well.

**2** Core the apples, leaving the skin on. Peel the lime, don't worry about the pips.

**3** Add all the fruit, vegetables & basil to the NUTRiBULLET tall cup. Make sure the ingredients do not go past the MAX line on your machine.

**4** Add water, again being careful not to exceed the MAX line.

**5** Twist on the NUTRiBULLET blade and blend until smooth.

### CHEF'S NOTE
Optional Nutriboost: Add 1 tablespoon of fresh almonds.

# SWEET PEPPER & PINEAPPLE BLAST

## Ingredients

- 2 handfuls of spinach
- 1 orange or yellow pepper
- 1 banana
- 200g/7oz fresh peeled pineapple
- Water

## Method

1 Rinse the ingredients well.

2 De-seed the pepper, removing and discarding the stalk.

3 Peel the banana and break into three pieces.

4 Add all the fruit & vegetables to the NUTRiBULLET tall cup. Make sure the ingredients do not go past the MAX line on your machine.

5 Add water, again being careful not to exceed the MAX line.

6 Twist on the NUTRiBULLET blade and blend until smooth.

## CHEF'S NOTE

Orange or yellow peppers tend to be the sweetest but use whatever you have to hand.

# BEST BANANA & COCONUT BLAST

## Ingredients

**CLEANSING JUICE** ➡

- 2 handfuls of spinach
- 1 banana
- 200g/7oz fresh peeled pineapple
- 250ml/1 cup coconut water

## Method

**1** Rinse the ingredients well.

**2** Peel the banana and break into three pieces.

**3** Add the fruit, vegetables & coconut water to the NUTRiBULLET tall cup. Make sure the ingredients do not go past the MAX line on your machine.

**4** Twist on the NUTRiBULLET blade and blend until smooth.

### CHEF'S NOTE
Use as much coconut water as you need to reach the max line.

# GOOD GREENS BLAST

## Ingredients

- 2 handfuls of spinach
- 1 apple
- 1 avocado
- 125g/4oz tenderstem broccoli
- Water

## Method

1 Rinse the ingredients well.

2 Core the apple, leaving the skin on.

3 Scoop out the avocado flesh, discarding the stone and skin.

4 Add all the fruit & vegetables to the NUTRiBULLET tall cup. Make sure the ingredients do not go past the MAX line on your machine.

5 Add water, again being careful not to exceed the MAX line.

6 Twist on the NUTRiBULLET blade and blend until smooth.

### CHEF'S NOTE

Try adding a dash of lemon or lime to this Nutriblast.

51

# SMOOTH & NUTTY BLAST

**SERVES 1**
NUTRiBLAST

## Ingredients

**HEART PROTECTOR** ➜

- 2 handfuls of spinach
- 2 bananas
- 125g/4oz fresh peeled pineapple
- 1 handful fresh cashew nuts
- Water

## Method

**1** Rinse the ingredients well.

**2** Peel the bananas and break each into three pieces.

**3** Add all the fruit & vegetables to the NUTRiBULLET tall cup. Make sure the ingredients do not go past the MAX line on your machine.

**4** Add water, again being careful not to exceed the MAX line.

**5** Twist on the NUTRiBULLET blade and blend until smooth.

### CHEF'S NOTE
Optional Nutriboost: Add 1 teaspoon of flax or chia seeds.

# Skinny
# GREEN
# SMOOTHIES

# SIMPLY SPINACH

## Ingredients

- 3 handfuls of spinach
- 1 apple
- ½ cucumber

- ½ lemon
- Water

## Method

**1** Rinse the ingredients well.

**2** Core the apple, leaving the skin on. Top the cucumber, leaving the skin on.

**3** Peel the lemon, don't worry about the pips.

**4** Add the fruit & vegetables to the NUTRiBULLET tall cup. Make sure the ingredients do not go past the MAX line on your machine.

**5** Add water, again being careful not to exceed the MAX line.

**6** Twist on the NUTRiBULLET blade and blend until smooth.

### CHEF'S NOTE
Optional Nutriboost: add 1 tablespoon of pumpkin seeds.

# GENTLE DETOX

## Ingredients

**BRAIN BUILDER** →

- 2 handfuls of spinach
- 1 handful of kale
- 2 apples
- ½ lemon
- Water

## Method

**1** Rinse the ingredients well.

**2** Core the apples, leaving the skin on. Peel the lemon, don't worry about the pips.

**3** Add the fruit & vegetables to the NUTRiBULLET tall cup. Make sure the ingredients do not go past the MAX line on your machine.

**4** Add water, again being careful not to exceed the MAX line.

**5** Twist on the NUTRiBULLET blade and blend until smooth.

## CHEF'S NOTE

Optional Nutriboost: add 2 teaspoons of sesame seeds.

# SWEET KALE

## Ingredients

- 3 handfuls of kale
- 1 apple
- 100g/3½oz fresh peeled pineapple
- Water

## Method

**1** Rinse the ingredients well.

**2** Core the apple, leaving the skin on.

**3** Add the fruit & vegetables to the NUTRiBULLET tall cup. Make sure the ingredients do not go past the MAX line on your machine.

**4** Add water, again being careful not to exceed the MAX line.

**5** Twist on the NUTRiBULLET blade and blend until smooth.

## CHEF'S NOTE
Optional Nutriboost: add 1 tablespoon of sunflower seeds.

# SPINACH HERB GARDEN

## Ingredients

**HEALING HERBS** →

- 3 handfuls of spinach
- 1 small handful of fresh mint
- 1 small handful of fresh basil
- 1 apple
- ½ cucumber
- Water

## Method

1 Rinse the ingredients well.

2 Core the apple, leaving the skin on. Top the cucumber, leaving the skin on.

3 Add the fruit & vegetables to the NUTRiBULLET tall cup. Make sure the ingredients do not go past the MAX line on your machine.

4 Add water, again being careful not to exceed the MAX line.

5 Twist on the NUTRiBULLET blade and blend until smooth.

### CHEF'S NOTE
Optional Nutriboost: add 1 tablespoon of fresh almonds.

# LIGHT CELERY SNAP

**SERVES 1**
NUTRiBLAST

## Ingredients

- 2 celery stalks
- ½ cucumber
- 2 handfuls of spinach

- 1 vine ripened tomato
- Water

## Method

**1** Rinse the ingredients well.

**2** Top the celery stalks and cucumber, leaving the skin on the cucumber.

**3** Add the fruit & vegetables to the NUTRiBULLET tall cup. Make sure the ingredients do not go past the MAX line on your machine.

**4** Add water, again being careful not to exceed the MAX line.

**5** Twist on the NUTRiBULLET blade and blend until smooth.

### CHEF'S NOTE
Optional Nutriboost: add 2 teaspoons of hemp seeds.

# CUCUMBER CLEANSER

## Ingredients

**ANTIOXIDANT**

- 1 whole cucumber
- 1 celery stalk
- 2 handfuls of spinach
- 1 apple
- ½ lemon
- Water

## Method

**1** Top and tail the cucumber and celery, leaving the skin on the cucumber.

**2** Core the apple, leaving the skin on. Peel the lemon, don't worry about the pips.

**3** Add the fruit & vegetables to the NUTRiBULLET tall cup. Make sure the ingredients do not go past the MAX line on your machine.

**4** Add water, again being careful not to exceed the MAX line.

**5** Twist on the NUTRiBULLET blade and blend until smooth.

### CHEF'S NOTE
Optional Nutriboost: add 1 teaspoon of chia seeds.

# KALE & CHIA TONIC

## Ingredients

- 2 handfuls of kale
- 2 apples
- 120ml/½ cup coconut water
- 2 tsp chia seeds
- Water

## Method

**1** Rinse the ingredients well.

**2** Core the apples, leaving the skin on.

**3** Add the kale, apples, coconut water & chia seeds to the NUTRiBULLET tall cup. Make sure the ingredients do not go past the MAX line on your machine.

**4** Add water (if there's space), again being careful not to exceed the MAX line.

**5** Twist on the NUTRiBULLET blade and blend until smooth.

## CHEF'S NOTE
Use regular water if you don't have coconut water.

# SPRING GREEN PEARS

## Ingredients

**FIBRE SOURCE** →

- 2 handfuls of spring greens
- 2 pears
- ½ cucumber
- Water

## Method

**1** Rinse the ingredients well.

**2** Core the pears, leaving the skin on. Top the cucumber, leaving the skin on.

**3** Add the fruit & vegetables to the NUTRiBULLET tall cup. Make sure the ingredients do not go past the MAX line on your machine.

**4** Add water, again being careful not to exceed the MAX line.

**5** Twist on the NUTRiBULLET blade and blend until smooth.

### CHEF'S NOTE
Optional Nutriboost: add 1 tablespoon sunflower seeds.

# KALE & AVOCADO BOOST

## Ingredients

- 2 handfuls of kale
- 1 apple
- 1 avocado
- Water

## Method

**1** Rinse the ingredients well.

**2** Core the apple, leaving the skin on. Scoop out the avocado flesh discarding the stone and rind.

**3** Add the fruit & vegetables to the NUTRiBULLET tall cup. Make sure the ingredients do not go past the MAX line on your machine.

**4** Add water, again being careful not to exceed the MAX line.

**5** Twist on the NUTRiBULLET blade and blend until smooth.

### CHEF'S NOTE
Optional Nutriboost: add 1 tablespoon of goji berries.

# HEALTHY GINGER BLAST

## Ingredients

**IMMUNITY BUILDER**

- 3 handfuls of spinach
- 2cm/1 inch fresh ginger root
- 1 pear
- ½ cucumber
- ½ lemon
- Water

## Method

**1** Rinse the ingredients well.

**2** Core the pear, leaving the skin on. Top the cucumber, leaving the skin on.

**3** Peel the lemon, don't worry about the pips.

**4** Add the fruit, vegetables & ginger to the NUTRiBULLET tall cup. Make sure the ingredients do not go past the MAX line on your machine.

**5** Add water, again being careful not to exceed the MAX line.

**6** Twist on the NUTRiBULLET blade and blend until smooth.

### CHEF'S NOTE
Fresh ginger aids the immune system so add as much as your palate can handle!

# MIXED GREEN MEDLEY

## Ingredients

- 1 handful of spinach
- 1 handful of kale
- 1 handful of Swiss chard
- 1 apple
- ½ lime
- 1 stalk of celery
- Water

## Method

**1** Rinse the ingredients well.

**2** Core the apple, leaving the skin on. Peel the lime, don't worry about the pips.

**3** Add the fruit & vegetables to the NUTRiBULLET tall cup. Make sure the ingredients do not go past the MAX line on your machine.

**4** Add water, again being careful not to exceed the MAX line.

**5** Twist on the NUTRiBULLET blade and blend until smooth.

### CHEF'S NOTE
Adjust the lime quantity to suit you own taste.

# CITRUS GREENS

## Ingredients

VITAMIN 'C'

- 3 handfuls of spinach
- 1 banana
- ½ lemon
- 1 orange
- Water

## Method

**1** Rinse the ingredients well.

**2** Peel the banana and break into three pieces.

**3** Peel the lemon and orange, don't worry about the pips.

**4** Add the fruit & vegetables to the NUTRiBULLET tall cup. Make sure the ingredients do not go past the MAX line on your machine.

**5** Add water, again being careful not to exceed the MAX line.

**6** Twist on the NUTRiBULLET blade and blend until smooth.

## CHEF'S NOTE

Optional Nutriboost: add 1 tablespoon of fresh, shelled walnuts.

# GREEN NUT MILK

## Ingredients

- 3 handfuls of spinach
- 1 banana
- 100g/3½oz fresh peeled pineapple
- 1 cup/250ml almond milk

## Method

**1** Rinse the ingredients well.

**2** Peel the banana and break into three pieces.

**3** Add the fruit & vegetables to the NUTRiBULLET tall cup. Make sure the ingredients do not go past the MAX line on your machine.

**4** Twist on the NUTRiBULLET blade and blend until smooth.

## CHEF'S NOTE
Add some water if you need to loosen this smoothie a little.

# STRAWBERRY & SPINACH TONIC

## Ingredients

**MEMORY BOOSTER!** →

- 2 handfuls of spinach
- 1 apple
- 1 banana
- 200g/7oz strawberries
- Water

## Method

**1** Rinse the ingredients well.

**2** Core the apple, leaving the skin on. Peel the banana and break into three pieces.

**3** Remove any green tops from the strawberries.

**4** Add the fruit & vegetables to the NUTRiBULLET tall cup. Make sure the ingredients do not go past the MAX line on your machine.

**5** Add water, again being careful not to exceed the MAX line.

**6** Twist on the NUTRiBULLET blade and blend until smooth.

### CHEF'S NOTE
Optional Nutriboost: add 2 teaspoons of hemp seeds.

# GOOD & GREEN

## Ingredients

- 3 handfuls of spinach
- 1 Pear
- 2 apples
- 1 cucumber
- Water

## Method

**1** Rinse the ingredients well.

**2** Core the pear & apples, leaving the skin on.

**3** Top and tail the cucumber, leaving the skin on.

**4** Add the fruit & vegetables to the NUTRiBULLET tall cup. Make sure the ingredients do not go past the MAX line on your machine.

**5** Add water, again being careful not to exceed the MAX line.

**6** Twist on the NUTRiBULLET blade and blend until smooth.

### CHEF'S NOTE
Optional Nutriboost: add 2 tablespoon of acai berries.

# ROMAINE KALE BLEND

## Ingredients

**HIGH IN CALCIUM**

- 1 handful of kale
- 2 handfuls of shredded romaine lettuce
- 2 green apples
- ½ lemon
- Water

## Method

**1** Rinse the ingredients well.

**2** Core the apples, leaving the skin on. Peel the lemon, don't worry about the pips.

**3** Add the fruit & vegetables to the NUTRiBULLET tall cup. Make sure the ingredients do not go past the MAX line on your machine.

**4** Add water, again being careful not to exceed the MAX line.

**5** Twist on the NUTRiBULLET blade and blend until smooth.

### CHEF'S NOTE
Optional Nutriboost: add 1 handful of fresh almonds.

# CHILLI GREENS

## Ingredients

- 1 handful of kale
- 2 handfuls of spinach
- 200g/7oz fresh pineapple

- ½ green chilli
- Water

## Method

**1** Rinse the ingredients well.

**2** De-seed the chilli.

**3** Add the fruit & vegetables to the NUTRiBULLET tall cup. Make sure the ingredients do not go past the MAX line on your machine.

**4** Add water, again being careful not to exceed the MAX line.

**5** Twist on the NUTRiBULLET blade and blend until smooth.

### CHEF'S NOTE
Adjust the fresh chilli quantity to suit your own taste.

# BROCCOLI BLAST

## Ingredients

**DETOX JUICE**

- 250g/9oz tenderstem broccoli
- 1 apple
- 2 carrots
- Water

## Method

**1** Rinse the ingredients well.

**2** Core the apple, leaving the skin on.

**3** Scrub and top the carrots, leaving the skin on.

**4** Add the fruit & vegetables to the NUTRiBULLET tall cup. Make sure the ingredients do not go past the MAX line on your machine.

**5** Add water, again being careful not to exceed the MAX line.

**6** Twist on the NUTRiBULLET blade and blend until smooth.

### CHEF'S NOTE
Optional Nutriboost: add 1 handful of cashew nuts.

# SALAD SMOOTHIE

## Ingredients

- 2 handfuls of shredded romaine lettuces
- 1 cucumber
- 1 green pepper
- ½ lemon
- 1 vine ripened tomato
- Water

## Method

**1** Rinse the ingredients well.

**2** Top and tail the cucumber, leaving the skin on.

**3** De-seed the pepper and discard the stalk. Peel the lemon, don't worry about the pips.

**4** Add the fruit & vegetables to the NUTRiBULLET tall cup. Make sure the ingredients do not go past the MAX line on your machine.

**5** Add water, again being careful not to exceed the MAX line.

**6** Twist on the NUTRiBULLET blade and blend until smooth.

## CHEF'S NOTE
Use a sweet orange or yellow pepper if you prefer.

# ASPARAGUS HIT

## Ingredients

**NUTRIENT RICH** →

- 200g/7oz asparagus tips
- 2 handfuls of spinach
- 2 carrots
- Water

## Method

**1** Rinse the ingredients well.

**2** Scrub and top the carrots, leaving the skin on.

**3** Add the vegetables to the NUTRiBULLET tall cup. Make sure the ingredients do not go past the MAX line on your machine.

**4** Add water, again being careful not to exceed the MAX line.

**5** Twist on the NUTRiBULLET blade and blend until smooth.

### CHEF'S NOTE
Optional Nutriboost: add 1 tablespoon of pumpkin seeds.

# CHINESE GREENS

## Ingredients

**AIDS DIGESTION**

- 1 fresh pak choi
- 1 pear
- 1 apple
- ½ lemon
- Water

## Method

**1** Rinse the ingredients well.

**2** Core the pear & apple, leaving the skin on. Peel the lemon, don't worry about the pips.

**3** Add the fruit & vegetables to the NUTRiBULLET tall cup. Make sure the ingredients do not go past the MAX line on your machine.

**4** Add water, again being careful not to exceed the MAX line.

**5** Twist on the NUTRiBULLET blade and blend until smooth.

### CHEF'S NOTE
Pak Choi is a Chinese cabbage widely available in most stores.

# Skinny
# WEIGHT LOSS
# SMOOTHIES

# SPICY TOMATO JUICE

## Ingredients

**SKIN CLEANSER** →

- 3 vine-ripened tomatoes
- 2 celery stalks
- 1 cucumber
- ½ fresh red chilli
- Water

## Method

**1** Rinse the ingredients well.

**2** Remove any green stalks from the tomatoes. Top and tail the cucumber, leaving the skin on.

**3** De-seed and chop the chilli.

**4** Add the fruit & vegetables to the NUTRiBULLET tall cup. Make sure the ingredients do not go past the MAX line on your machine.

**5** Add water, again being careful not to exceed the MAX line.

**6** Twist on the NUTRiBULLET blade and blend until smooth.

### CHEF'S NOTE
Use chilli powder if you don't have fresh chillies.

# CARROT ROCKET JUICE

## Ingredients

- 2-3 carrots
- 1 handful of spinach
- 2 handfuls of rocket leaves
- Water

## Method

**1** Rinse the ingredients well.

**2** Scrub and top the carrots, leaving the skin on.

**3** Add the vegetables & rocket to the NUTRiBULLET tall cup. Make sure the ingredients do not go past the MAX line on your machine.

**4** Add water, again being careful not to exceed the MAX line.

**5** Twist on the NUTRiBULLET blade and blend until smooth.

### CHEF'S NOTE
Rocket has a natural peppery flavour which gives this juice a gentle kick.

# GRAPE BERRY JUICE

**SERVES 1**
NUTRiBLAST

## Ingredients

**MEMORY BUILDER!**

- 1 apple
- 200g/7oz green seedless grapes
- 100g/3½oz blueberries
- Water

## Method

**1** Rinse the ingredients well.

**2** Core the apple, leaving the skin on. Remove any stalks from the grapes.

**3** Add all the fruit to the NUTRiBULLET tall cup. Make sure the ingredients do not go past the MAX line on your machine.

**4** Add water, again being careful not to exceed the MAX line.

**5** Twist on the NUTRiBULLET blade and blend until smooth.

### CHEF'S NOTE
Optional Nutriblast: add 1 handful of goji berries.

# GINGER APPLE JUICE

## Ingredients

- 2 apples
- 4cm/2inch piece of fresh ginger root
- ½ lemon
- Water

## Method

**1** Rinse the ingredients well.

**2** Core the apples, leaving the skin on. Peel the lemon, don't worry about the pips.

**3** Add all the fruit & ginger to the NUTRiBULLET tall cup. Make sure the ingredients do not go past the MAX line on your machine.

**4** Add water, again being careful not to exceed the MAX line.

**5** Twist on the NUTRiBULLET blade and blend until smooth.

### CHEF'S NOTE
Optional Nutriblast: add 2 teaspoons of hemp seeds.

# PINEAPPLE LEMON JUICE

## Ingredients

**AIDS DIGESTION!**

- 2 apples
- ½ lemon
- 200g/7oz fresh peeled pineapple
- Water

## Method

**1** Rinse the ingredients well.

**2** Core the apples, leaving the skin on. Peel the lemon, don't worry about the pips.

**3** Add all the fruit to the NUTRiBULLET tall cup. Make sure the ingredients do not go past the MAX line on your machine.

**4** Add water, again being careful not to exceed the MAX line.

**5** Twist on the NUTRiBULLET blade and blend until smooth.

### CHEF'S NOTE
Optional Nutriblast: add 2 teaspoons of pumpkin seeds.

# RUBY CELERY JUICE

## Ingredients

- 1 handful of spinach
- 2 celery stalks
- 1 carrot
- 1 medium beetroot
- Water

## Method

**1** Rinse the ingredients well.

**2** Scrub and top the carrot & beetroot, leaving the skin on.

**3** Add the fruit & vegetables to the NUTRiBULLET tall cup. Make sure the ingredients do not go past the MAX line on your machine.

**4** Add water, again being careful not to exceed the MAX line.

**5** Twist on the NUTRiBULLET blade and blend until smooth.

### CHEF'S NOTE
Fresh beetroot gives this juice a lovely ruby colour.

# GRAPEFRUIT & PINEAPPLE JUICE

## Ingredients

**VITAMIN 'C' RICH!**

- 1 grapefruit
- 1 apple
- 100g/3½oz fresh peeled pineapple
- Water

## Method

**1** Rinse the ingredients well.

**2** Peel the grapefruit and separate into segments, don't worry about the pips.
Core the apple, leaving the skin on.

**3** Add all the fruit to the NUTRiBULLET tall cup. Make sure the ingredients do not go past the MAX line on your machine.

**4** Add water, again being careful not to exceed the MAX line.

**5** Twist on the NUTRiBULLET blade and blend until smooth.

### CHEF'S NOTE
Optional Nutriblast: add 2 teaspoons of flax seeds.

# CITRUS MELON JUICE

## Ingredients

- ½ honeydew melon
- 1 lemon
- 1 apple
- Water

## Method

**1** Rinse the ingredients well.

**2** Scoop out the melon flesh, discarding the pips and rind.

**3** Peel the lemon, don't worry about the pips. Core the apple, leaving the skin on.

**4** Add all the fruit to the NUTRiBULLET tall cup. Make sure the ingredients do not go past the MAX line on your machine.

**5** Add water, again being careful not to exceed the MAX line.

**6** Twist on the NUTRiBULLET blade and blend until smooth.

## CHEF'S NOTE
Use lime if you prefer.

# KILLER KIWI JUICE

## Ingredients

VITAMIN 'E'

- 2 fresh kiwis
- 200g/7oz strawberries
- ½ lime
- Water

## Method

**1** Rinse the ingredients well.

**2** Peel the kiwis. Remove any green tops from the strawberries.

**3** Peel the lime, don't worry about the pips.

**4** Add all the fruit to the NUTRiBULLET tall cup. Make sure the ingredients do not go past the MAX line on your machine.

**5** Add water, again being careful not to exceed the MAX line.

**6** Twist on the NUTRiBULLET blade and blend until smooth.

## CHEF'S NOTE
This lovely juice is packed with vitamin C and antioxidants.

# AVOCADO FRUIT JUICE

## Ingredients

- 1 handful of spinach
- 1 apple
- ½ avocado

- ½ lime
- Water

## Method

**1** Rinse the ingredients well.

**2** Core the apple, leaving the skin on.

**3** Scoop out the avocado flesh discarding the stone and rind. Peel the lime, don't worry about the pips.

**4** Add all the fruit & vegetables to the NUTRiBULLET tall cup. Make sure the ingredients do not go past the MAX line on your machine.

**5** Add water, again being careful not to exceed the MAX line.

**6** Twist on the NUTRiBULLET blade and blend until smooth.

### CHEF'S NOTE
Optional Nutriblast: add 1 teaspoon of sesame seeds.

# Skinny
# SUPERFRUIT
# SMOOTHIES

# SPICED FRESH PEACH SMOOTHIE

## Ingredients

- 2 fresh peaches
- 1 pear
- 1 apple

- 1 banana
- ½ tsp ground cinnamon
- Water

## Method

**1** Rinse the ingredients well.

**2** De-stone the peaches, leaving the skin on.

**3** Core the pear and apple, leaving the skin on. Peel the banana and break into three pieces.

**4** Add the fruit & cinnamon to the NUTRiBULLET tall cup. Make sure the ingredients do not go past the MAX line on your machine.

**5** Add water, again being careful not to exceed the MAX line.

**6** Twist on the NUTRiBULLET blade and blend until smooth.

### CHEF'S NOTE
Optional Nutriboost: Add 1 teaspoon of flax seeds.

# MANGO & DOUBLE ALMOND SMOOTHIE

## Ingredients

**GOOD FATS** →

- 1 fresh mango
- 1 banana
- 120ml/½ cup almond milk
- 1 handful of fresh almonds
- Water

## Method

**1** Scoop out the mango flesh discarding the stone and skin.

**2** Peel the banana and break into three pieces.

**3** Add the fruit, milk & nuts to the NUTRiBULLET tall cup. Make sure the ingredients do not go past the MAX line on your machine.

**4** Add water (if there's space) again being careful not to exceed the MAX line.

**5** Twist on the NUTRiBULLET blade and blend until smooth.

### CHEF'S NOTE
Optional Nutriboost: Add 1 teaspoon of hemp seeds.

# KIWI & ORANGE SMOOTHIE

**SERVES 1**
NUTRiBLAST

## Ingredients

- 2 fresh kiwis
- 1 apple
- 1 banana

- 1 orange
- Water

## Method

**1** Rinse the ingredients well.

**2** Peel the kiwis. Core the apple, leaving the skin on.

**3** Peel the banana and break into three pieces.

**4** Peel the orange and divide into segments, don't worry about the pips.

**5** Add the fruit to the NUTRiBULLET tall cup. Make sure the ingredients do not go past the MAX line on your machine.

**6** Add water, again being careful not to exceed the MAX line.

**7** Twist on the NUTRiBULLET blade and blend until smooth.

### CHEF'S NOTE
Optional Nutriboost: Add 1 teaspoon of chia seeds.

# SIMPLE BERRY & PINEAPPLE SMOOTHIE

## Ingredients

**ENERGY PUNCH!**

- 250g/9oz fresh mixed berries
- 200g/7oz fresh peeled pineapple
- 1 banana
- Water

## Method

**1** Rinse the ingredients well.

**2** Peel the banana and break into three pieces.

**3** Add the fruit to the NUTRiBULLET tall cup. Make sure the ingredients do not go past the MAX line on your machine.

**4** Add water, again being careful not to exceed the MAX line.

**5** Twist on the NUTRiBULLET blade and blend until smooth.

### CHEF'S NOTE
This smoothie is also good with almond milk in place of water.

# BANANA & FIG SMOOTHIE

## Ingredients

- 2 bananas
- 200g/7oz dried figs
- 2 tsp runny honey

- 120ml/½ cup soy milk
- Water

## Method

**1** Rinse the ingredients well.

**2** Peel the banana and break into three pieces each.

**3** Add the fruit, honey & milk to the NUTRiBULLET tall cup. Make sure the ingredients do not go past the MAX line on your machine.

**3** Add water (if there's space), again being careful not to exceed the MAX line.

**4** Twist on the NUTRiBULLET blade and blend until smooth.

## CHEF'S NOTE

Optional Nutriboost: Add 1 tablespoon of goji berries.

# CHERRY APPLE SMOOTHIE

## Ingredients

**ANTI AGING!**

- 200g/7oz fresh cherries
- 2 apples
- 1 banana
- Water

## Method

**1** Rinse the ingredients well.

**2** Remove the stones and stalks from the cherries

**3** Core the apples, leaving the skin on. Peel the banana and break into three pieces.

**4** Add all the fruit to the NUTRiBULLET tall cup. Make sure the ingredients do not go past the MAX line on your machine.

**5** Add water, again being careful not to exceed the MAX line.

**6** Twist on the NUTRiBULLET blade and blend until smooth.

### CHEF'S NOTE
Leave out the banana for a thinner consistency.

# SWEET BLUEBERRY SMOOTHIE

## Ingredients

- 200g/7oz fresh blueberries
- 1 apple
- 1 banana
- 120ml/½ cup soy milk
- 1 handful fresh shelled walnuts
- Water

## Method

**1** Rinse the ingredients well.

**2** Core the apple, leaving the skin on. Peel the banana and break into three pieces.

**3** Add the fruit, milk & nuts to the NUTRiBULLET tall cup. Make sure the ingredients do not go past the MAX line on your machine.

**4** Add water (if there's space), again being careful not to exceed the MAX line.

**5** Twist on the NUTRiBULLET blade and blend until smooth.

### CHEF'S NOTE
Optional Nutriboost: Add 1 tablespoon of acai berries.

# PEAR & DATE SMOOTHIE

## Ingredients

**SOURCE OF FIBRE!**

- 2 pears
- 1 banana
- 200g/7oz pitted dates
- Water

## Method

**1** Rinse the ingredients well.

**2** Core the pears, leaving the skin on. Peel the banana and break into three pieces.

**3** Add the fruit to the NUTRiBULLET tall cup. Make sure the ingredients do not go past the MAX line on your machine.

**4** Add water, again being careful not to exceed the MAX line.

**5** Twist on the NUTRiBULLET blade and blend until smooth.

### CHEF'S NOTE
Make sure the dates are pitted as their stones will ruin the taste.

# EXTRA SMOOTH STRAWBERRIES

## Ingredients

- 1 avocado
- 1 banana
- 250g/9oz strawberries
- Water

## Method

**1** Rinse the ingredients well.

**2** Scoop out the avocado flesh, discarding the stone and rind.

**3** Peel the banana and break into three pieces. Discard the green tops off the strawberries.

**4** Add the fruit to the NUTRiBULLET tall cup. Make sure the ingredients do not go past the MAX line on your machine.

**5** Add water, again being careful not to exceed the MAX line.

**6** Twist on the NUTRiBULLET blade and blend until smooth.

## CHEF'S NOTE
The banana and avocado combine to make this super smooth. Add a little honey if you like.

# NUTTY PLUM SMOOTHIE

## Ingredients

**AIDS DIGESTION**

- 4 fresh plums
- 1 apple
- 1 banana
- 1-2 handfuls of fresh cashew nuts
- Water

## Method

**1** Rinse the ingredients well.

**2** De-stone the plums, leaving the skin on.

**3** Core the apple, leaving the skin on. Peel the banana and break into three pieces.

**4** Add the fruit & nuts to the NUTRiBULLET tall cup. Make sure the ingredients do not go past the MAX line on your machine.

**5** Add water, again being careful not to exceed the MAX line.

**6** Twist on the NUTRiBULLET blade and blend until smooth.

### CHEF'S NOTE
Optional Nutriboost: Add 1 teaspoon of flax seeds.

# Other COOKNATION TITLES

If you enjoyed 'The NUTRiBULLET Recipe Book' we'd really appreciate your feedback. Reviews help others decide if this is the right book for them so a moment of your time would be appreciated.

## Thank you.

You may also be interested in other '**Skinny**' titles in the CookNation series. You can find all the following great titles by searching under '**CookNation**'.

### THE SKINNY SLOW COOKER RECIPE BOOK

Delicious Recipes Under 300, 400 And 500 Calories.

**Paperback / eBook**

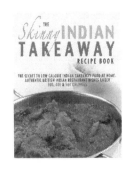

### THE SKINNY INDIAN TAKEAWAY RECIPE BOOK

Authentic British Indian Restaurant Dishes Under 300, 400 And 500 Calories. The Secret To Low Calorie Indian Takeaway Food At Home.

**Paperback / eBook**

### THE HEALTHY KIDS SMOOTHIE BOOK

40 Delicious Goodness In A Glass Recipes for Happy Kids.

**eBook**

### THE SKINNY 5:2 FAST DIET FAMILY FAVOURITES RECIPE BOOK

Eat With All The Family On Your Diet Fasting Days.

**Paperback / eBook**

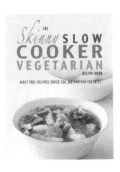

### THE SKINNY SLOW COOKER VEGETARIAN RECIPE BOOK

Delicious Recipes Under 200, 300 And 400 Calories.

**Paperback / eBook**

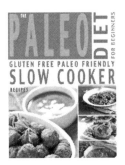

### THE PALEO DIET FOR BEGINNERS SLOW COOKER RECIPE BOOK

Gluten Free, Everyday Essential Slow Cooker Paleo Recipes For Beginners.

**eBook**

### THE SKINNY 5:2 SLOW COOKER RECIPE BOOK

Skinny Slow Cooker Recipe And Menu Ideas Under 100, 200, 300 & 400 Calories For Your 5:2 Diet.

**Paperback / eBook**

### THE SKINNY 5:2 BIKINI DIET RECIPE BOOK

Recipes & Meal Planners Under 100, 200 & 300 Calories. Get Ready For Summer & Lose Weight...FAST!

**Paperback / eBook**

### THE SKINNY 5:2 FAST DIET MEALS FOR ONE

Single Serving Fast Day Recipes & Snacks Under 100, 200 & 300 Calories.

**Paperback / eBook**

### THE SKINNY HALOGEN OVEN FAMILY FAVOURITES RECIPE BOOK

Healthy, Low Calorie Family Meal-Time Halogen Oven Recipes Under 300, 400 and 500 Calories.

**Paperback / eBook**

### THE SKINNY 5:2 FAST DIET VEGETARIAN MEALS FOR ONE

Single Serving Fast Day Recipes & Snacks Under 100, 200 & 300 Calories.

**Paperback / eBook**

### THE PALEO DIET FOR BEGINNERS MEALS FOR ONE

The Ultimate Paleo Single Serving Cookbook.

**Paperback / eBook**

### THE SKINNY SOUP MAKER RECIPE BOOK

Delicious Low Calorie, Healthy and Simple Soup Recipes Under 100, 200 and 300 Calories. Perfect For Any Diet and Weight Loss Plan.

**Paperback / eBook**

### THE PALEO DIET FOR BEGINNERS HOLIDAYS

Thanksgiving, Christmas & New Year Paleo Friendly Recipes.

**eBook**

### SKINNY HALOGEN OVEN COOKING FOR ONE

Single Serving, Healthy, Low Calorie Halogen Oven Recipes Under 200, 300 and 400 Calories.

**Paperback / eBook**

### SKINNY WINTER WARMERS RECIPE BOOK

Soups, Stews, Casseroles & One Pot Meals Under 300, 400 & 500 Calories.

**Paperback / eBook**

## THE SKINNY 5:2 DIET RECIPE BOOK COLLECTION

All The 5:2 Fast Diet Recipes You'll Ever Need. All Under 100, 200, 300, 400 And 500 Calories.

**eBook**

## THE SKINNY SLOW COOKER CURRY RECIPE BOOK

Low Calorie Curries From Around The World.

**Paperback / eBook**

## THE SKINNY BREAD MACHINE RECIPE BOOK

70 Simple, Lower Calorie, Healthy Breads...Baked To Perfection In Your Bread Maker.

**Paperback / eBook**

## MORE SKINNY SLOW COOKER RECIPES

75 More Delicious Recipes Under 300, 400 & 500 Calories.

**Paperback / eBook**

## THE SKINNY 5:2 DIET CHICKEN DISHES RECIPE BOOK

Delicious Low Calorie Chicken Dishes Under 300, 400 & 500 Calories.

**Paperback / eBook**

## THE SKINNY 5:2 CURRY RECIPE BOOK

Spice Up Your Fast Days With Simple Low Calorie Curries, Snacks, Soups, Salads & Sides Under 200, 300 & 400 Calories.

**Paperback / eBook**

## THE SKINNY JUICE DIET RECIPE BOOK

5lbs, 5 Days. The Ultimate Kick- Start Diet and Detox Plan to Lose Weight & Feel Great!

**Paperback / eBook**

## THE SKINNY SLOW COOKER SOUP RECIPE BOOK

Simple, Healthy & Delicious Low Calorie Soup Recipes For Your Slow Cooker. All Under 100, 200 & 300 Calories.

**Paperback / eBook**

## THE SKINNY SLOW COOKER SUMMER RECIPE BOOK

Fresh & Seasonal Summer Recipes For Your Slow Cooker. All Under 300, 400 And 500 Calories.

**Paperback / eBook**

## THE SKINNY HOT AIR FRYER COOKBOOK

Delicious & Simple Meals For Your Hot Air Fryer: Discover The Healthier Way To Fry.

**Paperback / eBook**

## THE SKINNY ACTIFRY COOKBOOK

Guilt-free and Delicious ActiFry Recipe Ideas: Discover The Healthier Way to Fry!

**Paperback / eBook**

## THE SKINNY ICE CREAM MAKER

Delicious Lower Fat, Lower Calorie Ice Cream, Frozen Yogurt & Sorbet Recipes For Your Ice Cream Maker.

**Paperback / eBook**

## THE SKINNY 15 MINUTE MEALS RECIPE BOOK

Delicious, Nutritious & Super-Fast Meals in 15 Minutes Or Less. All Under 300, 400 & 500 Calories.

**Paperback / eBook**

## THE SKINNY SLOW COOKER COLLECTION

5 Fantastic Books of Delicious, Diet-friendly Skinny Slow Cooker Recipes: ALL Under 200, 300, 400 & 500 Calories!

**eBook**

## THE SKINNY MEDITERRANEAN RECIPE BOOK

Simple, Healthy & Delicious Low Calorie Mediterranean Diet Dishes. All Under 200, 300 & 400 Calories.

**Paperback / eBook**

## THE SKINNY LOW CALORIE RECIPE BOOK

Great Tasting, Simple & Healthy Meals Under 300, 400 & 500 Calories. Perfect For Any Calorie Controlled Diet.

**Paperback / eBook**

## THE SKINNY TAKEAWAY RECIPE BOOK

Healthier Versions Of Your Fast Food Favourites: All Under 300, 400 & 500 Calories.

**Paperback / eBook**

## THE SKINNY NUTRIBULLET RECIPE BOOK

80+ Delicious & Nutritious Healthy Smoothie Recipes. Burn Fat, Lose Weight and Feel Great!

**Paperback / eBook**

## THE SKINNY NUTRIBULLET SOUP RECIPE BOOK

Delicious, Quick & Easy, Single Serving Soups & Pasta Sauces For Your Nutribullet. All Under 100, 200, 300 & 400 Calories!

**Paperback / eBook**

8421167R00060

Printed in Great Britain
by Amazon.co.uk, Ltd.,
Marston Gate.